EYEWITNESS EXPLORER

ROCK & FOSSIL HUNTER

by Ben Morgan
US Consultant Richard H. Efthim, Naturalist Center Manager
at the National Museum of Natural History, Smithsonian Institution
UK Consultant Dr. Douglas Palmer

SMITHSONIAN

Penguin
Random
House

Produced for Dorling Kindersley Ltd by
Cooling Brown Ltd
Creative Director Arthur Brown
Editor Helen Ridge
Designers Tish Jones, Elly King, Elaine Hewson, Mick Barratt

For Dorling Kindersley Ltd
Senior Editors Fran Baines, Carey Scott
Senior Art Editor Stefan Podhorodecki
Managing Editor Linda Esposito
Managing Art Editor Jane Thomas
Publishing Managers Caroline Buckingham, Andrew Macintyre
Jacket Designer Chris Drew
Jacket Copywriter Adam Powley
Jacket Editor Carrie Love
Art Director Simon Webb
Publishing Director Jonathan Metcalf
Production Controller Erica Rosen
Picture Researcher Liz Moore
DK Picture Library Sarah Mills
DTP Designer Natasha Lu
Photography Dave King

REVISED EDITION
Project Art Editor Deep Shikha Walia
Editor Suneha Dutta
Art Editors Mary Sandberg, Shipra Jain, Shreya Sadhan
Senior Editors Carron Brown, Shatarupa Chaudhuri
DTP Designer Pawan Kumar
Senior DTP Designer Harish Aggarwal
Managing Editors Linda Esposito, Alka Thakur Hazarika
Managing Art Editors Michael Duffy, Romi Chakraborty
CTS Manager Balwant Singh
Publisher Andrew Macintyre
Producer, Pre-production Lucy Sims
Senior Producer Gemma Sharpe
Jacket Editors Claire Gell, Maud Whatley
Jacket Designers Laura Brim, Dhirendra Singh
Managing Jacket Editor Saloni Singh
Jacket Development Manager Sophia MTT
Publishing Director Jonathan Metcalf
Associate Publishing Director Liz Wheeler
Art Director Phil Ormerod

SMITHSONIAN ENTERPRISES
Product Development Manager Kealy Wilson
Licensing Manager Ellen Nanney
Vice President, Education and Consumer Products Brigid Ferraro
**Senior Vice President, Education
and Consumer Products** Carol LeBlanc
President Chris Liedel

First American Edition, 2005
This American Edition, 2015
Published in the United States by
DK Publishing, 345 Hudson Street
New York, New York 10014

A catalog record record for this book is available
from the Library of Congress.
ISBN 978-1-4654-3015-1

DK books are available at special discounts when purchased in bulk
for sales promotions, premiums, fund-raising, or educational use.
For details, contact: DK Publishing Special Markets, 345 Hudson Street,
New York, New York 10014
SpecialSales@dk.com

Printed and bound in China by Hung Hing
Color reproduction by Alta Image Ltd, London, UK

Contents

A world of rock

Rock is the main ingredient in planet Earth. Nearly everything under your feet is rock. It may be buried out of sight, but it's always there. Rocks are full of surprises and secrets. They give us precious gems, gold, and vital resources such as iron and glass. Written into rock is a record of Earth's fascinating history, preserved as fossils.

Giant's Causeway

At the Giant's Causeway in Northern Ireland, pillars of rock run like stepping stones into the sea. They formed 60 million years ago when lava solidified into a type of rock called basalt.

This microscopic view shows interlocking crystals of the minerals that make up basalt rock

THIRD ROCK FROM THE SUN

After Earth formed 4.5 billion years ago, it became hot and molten. The heaviest materials, such as iron, mostly sank to the center, while lighter materials, such as rock-forming minerals, floated to the top. As a result, Earth now has a layered structure, like a soft-boiled egg. In the center is a hot, partly liquid core of iron. Around the core is a deep layer of hot, soft rock (the mantle), and around that is a brittle crust of cold, hardened rock, like an eggshell.

Crust

Hot, soft rock (mantle)

Molten core

Inside Earth ▶
Planet Earth is a gigantic ball of rock and metal. Most of the metal is in the core, and most of the rock is in the outer layers.

◄ What is rock?

A typical rock is a mixture of solid chemicals called minerals, which are pressed tightly together like puzzle pieces. If you look closely, you can sometimes see the separate minerals as grains (small crystals) in a rock. Most rocks are hard and brittle, but some crumble to powder when you rub them.

Malachite

▲ What is a mineral?

Minerals are naturally occurring solids that are inorganic (not from living things) and usually made of crystals. Ice is a mineral because it fits this definition. So are the tiny, shiny grains in sand, which consist of the mineral quartz. There are thousands of different minerals, including diamond, gold, and salt. Most rocks are made of a limited range, called the rock-forming minerals.

Tourmaline crystals

What is a crystal? ▲

A crystal is a solid chemical with a regular, geometrical shape. Crystals typically have smooth, flat faces that meet in sharp edges. They often look shiny or glassy. Their shape comes from the regular arrangement of atoms inside the crystal. In many rocks the crystals are too small to see, but they are there, nevertheless, by the thousands. In rare cases, crystals may grow as large as telephone poles.

Tyrannosaurus skull

What is a fossil? ►

A fossil is a relic of a living thing that died thousands, or millions, of years ago. Most fossils are remains of creatures that no longer exist, such as dinosaurs. Hard parts of their bodies, such as bones, were buried. Over time, minerals replaced these organic materials, turning them into rock. Some fossils, such as footprints, are merely impressions.

Rock types

Scientists can classify almost all rocks into one of three main types, depending on how the rocks form. The types are known as igneous rock, sedimentary rock, and metamorphic rock. Over millions of years, each type can slowly change into one of the others in an endless process called the rock cycle.

Pink granite

Basalt

Sandstone

Igneous rock

About 90 percent of the rock in Earth's crust is igneous. Igneous rock forms when molten rock cools and solidifies. When this happens underground, the molten rock (magma) solidifies slowly, giving crystals time to form. The magma becomes a hard, crystalline rock with large grains, such as granite. Igneous rock can also form on Earth's surface when lava escapes from a volcano. The lava solidifies quickly, especially if it flows into water, as in the picture below. It forms rock with no, or very tiny, visible crystals, such as basalt.

Lava flowing into the sea, Hawaii

Sedimentary rock

Sand, mud, and even the remains of living organisms can all turn into rock. These sediments settle on the sea floor, building up in layers. Over time, deep layers are compressed by the weight of the sediment on top, and water seeping through the layers deposits minerals that glue the sediment particles together. As a result, the sediment becomes sedimentary rock. Limestone, shale, and sandstone all form this way. The layers are sometimes visible as horizontal bands called strata.

Vermilion Cliffs, Utah

The rock cycle

The rock in Earth's crust is continually being destroyed and recycled. Rock on the surface is worn down to fragments and eventually settles to become sedimentary rock. Rock underground is melted to form igneous rock, or squashed and cooked, by the heat of molten rock to form metamorphic rock. Movements in Earth's crust lift underground rock back to the surface.

Rivers wash sediment into the sea

Ice and rain eat away at mountains

Lava builds up into new mountains

Underground rock layers are crushed and folded by pressure

Sediment builds up on the sea floor

Molten rock oozes back to the surface

Heat from molten rock transforms the surrounding rock

Mylonite

Metamorphic rock

Deep underground, rock can be subjected to intense heat and pressure. These forces, while not melting the rock outright, can cause minerals to recrystallize in new forms. The result is a hard, crystalline type of rock called metamorphic rock, which frequently has wavy or stripy patterns. Metamorphic rock often forms in mountainous regions, where Earth's crust is buckling and folding under tremendous pressure. Examples include marble, slate, and mylonite.

Mount McKinley, Alaska

THE MOVING CRUST

Although it looks rock solid, Earth's crust is moving. The crust is glued to the mantle below, and the mantle churns slowly about like very thick syrup. As a result, the crust has broken into huge fragments called plates. In some places, molten rock seeps up between the fragments and pushes them apart. In other places, two plates crunch together, and the weaker plate is forced deep underground, where the rock heats up and melts. These movements keep the rock in Earth's crust moving in an endless cycle.

Mantle

Earth's crust is broken into plates

Safety and equipment

You don't need any special gear to start learning about rocks and fossils, but the equipment on this page may be useful. If you go hunting for rocks and fossils, take the following safety precautions: wear highly visible clothing and make sure an adult accompanies you; don't climb cliffs or enter working quarries, and avoid the base of cliffs after storms. If you visit the coast, check tide times and avoid places that are dangerous when the tide comes in.

▲ Hand lens
A x10 hand lens helps expert rock collectors to identify their finds by inspecting the grain. It isn't essential for beginners.

Protective goggles

Safety hat and gloves

◄ Boots
Wear sturdy boots with ankle protection when walking on rough or rocky ground. Wear waterproof boots in wet or muddy places.

Brightly colored safety hats are best

Safety equipment ▶
A hard hat is essential anywhere with a risk of rock falls, such as a quarry or cliff base. Wear strong fabric gloves for handling rough or sharp material. If you stand near someone who's using a rock hammer, wear safety goggles. Hard hats, fabric gloves, and safety goggles can all be bought from hardware stores.

Wear rubber or plastic gloves when handling chemicals

HANDLING CHEMICALS

Some activities in this book involve chemicals that must not touch your eyes, mouth, and skin. When using such chemicals, wear protective gloves and goggles. Don't touch your eyes or lips while wearing the gloves. Afterward, throw away disposable gloves and wash your hands thoroughly. Read the manufacturer's instructions before using crystal kits, modeling resin, or plaster of Paris, and make sure you have adult supervision at all times. The symbol above appears when adult supervision is required.

Map and compass ▸
A map and compass will help you to find your site, and can give you an exact reference for the location. It is very important to record the location of rock, fossil, and mineral finds for future reference.

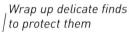

It's best to keep maps in waterproof wallets

A rock hammer is useful for breaking up large rocks

Rock hammer ▸
A rock, or geological, hammer is very useful for splitting rocks or breaking fossils away from bedrock. Only adults should use them, and a carpenter's hammer should never be used instead because the metal head may splinter. Protective goggles should always be worn by the person using the rock hammer, and by anyone nearby, because rock splinters can fly off in any direction.

◂ Penknife
A penknife is handy for prying rocks and fossils, scratching off dirt, or identifying minerals by the scratch test (see page 26).

◂ Trowel
A trowel is used for carefully scraping away mud or other soft sediment. When used properly, the edge of the trowel will catch solid items, such as flints, or fossils buried in the mud.

Wrap up delicate finds to protect them

Use sample bags and containers that can be sealed

Wrapping materials ▸
Fossils can be surprisingly delicate—wrap them in newspaper, bubble wrap, or cloth. Small plastic bags or containers are useful for tiny specimens.

Notepad and pen
When you find an interesting rock or fossil, write down the location with a notepad and pen. Do this when you make a find, not when you get home. Keep the note wrapped with the specimen.

BUYING ROCKS AND FOSSILS
Many collectors buy rocks, minerals, or fossils from specialty shops as well as collecting them in the field. You can also buy cheap rocks and fossils over the Internet, but be sure you know what you're buying, since minerals are toxic. Only buy fossils from reputable suppliers—some of the best-looking commercial fossils are fakes.

Cut and polished agates

Become a rock hound

Hunting for rocks is enormous fun—nothing beats the excitement of discovering rare minerals or shiny crystals with your own eyes. All that you really need to become a rock hound is a pair of sharp eyes and a bit of patience. It also helps if you plan your trips in advance—if you know where to look, your hunts will be much more fruitful.

Hand lens

WHAT YOU WILL NEED

- Bag for collecting rocks
- Water
- Dishpan
- Scrub brush
- Penknife
- Bleach
- Magnifying glass

Bleach is poisonous, so use only with adult supervision.

IMPORTANT

To be a good rock hound, you need to follow certain safety procedures. See pages 8–9 for guidance.

On the beach
A beach is a good place to look for interesting rocks.

1 Walk slowly as you look at the ground and collect as many different types of rock as you can: hard, soft, smooth, shiny, rough, crumbly, flat, and so on. If you're with a friend, take the rainbow challenge: see who can find the most colors. Put the best small specimens in a bag. Don't worry if they're dirty—you can clean them at home.

Stromatolite

Shelly limestone

Obsidian

WHERE TO COLLECT ROCKS

There are two different kinds of site where interesting rocks are easy to find: outcrops and deposits. Outcrops are places such as cliffs and quarries, where the bedrock that normally lies hidden below ground is exposed. Deposits are places where small, loose stones collect, such as beaches, river beds, and fields.

◄ River beds
Hard-wearing stones accumulate as gravel in rivers and streams. If you're very lucky, you might find gemstones among the gravel.

CODE OF CONDUCT

Remember to behave sensibly when collecting rocks and minerals. Always seek permission before entering, or collecting rocks from, private land. A rock hammer should be used as little as possible, and only by an adult. Don't use it in protected areas, such as national parks. Wherever possible, collect from fallen rocks, rubble, or scree rather than hammering outcrops. If you open any gates, close them behind you. Don't leave litter or disturb animals, and don't collect rocks from walls or buildings.

▲ **On the hunt**
It's better to collect loose, fallen rock than hammering outcrops, but don't climb rubbly slopes like this one—they are dangerous.

2 **Clean the rocks** when you get home. Brush off loose dirt, or scrape it off with a penknife. Then wash the rocks in warm water with a little detergent. Use a scrub brush to remove dirt, or leave very dirty rocks to soak overnight. If a rock has a green stain caused by algae, ask an adult to soak it in water containing a dash of bleach.

3 **Leave the rocks to dry,** then inspect them with a magnifying glass. Can you see individual grains or crystals? Feel the rocks carefully to see which ones are hard or crumbly. The rocks you've collected will be very useful for the activities in this book. You can also use them to start a collection (see page 14).

Use a scrub brush to remove mud and grit from your rocks

Rock stars

You don't have to go to the country to see rocks—just take a stroll in town. When you know how to spot granite, sandstone, and limestone, you'll see them in buildings everywhere. Throughout history, people have used rocks to build with. Usually, they made do with local rocks, but sometimes they looked farther afield. As the structures on this page show, the rocks often tell a fascinating story.

Stonehenge ▲
The builders of Stonehenge in England used a Welsh rock called dolerite. Unless the rock had been carried to England by glaciers, the builders must have dragged each rock 155 miles (250 km).

The Pyramids ▶
The pyramids in Egypt are made largely of fossils. They were built with a rock called nummulitic limestone, which formed 50 million years ago from the shells of small sea organisms. It took 30,000 men at least 20 years to build the biggest pyramid. It was the world's tallest building for 4,000 years.

RECYCLED ROCK

Building materials such as bricks, cement, and concrete are all recycled rock. Bricks come from clay that is shaped into blocks and cooked or dried in the sun to harden. Cement and plaster are made with minerals, such as calcite and gypsum, which are heated to drive out water and then powdered. When water is added, crystals form and make them set solid. Concrete is a mass of cement and pebbles.

Making bricks ▶
These Indian villagers are making clay bricks. Clay forms when the minerals in rocks such as granite rot and crumble. Rivers wash away the clay, which then settles as mud.

The marble is inlaid with sapphires and other precious stones

◄ Taj Mahal
An Indian emperor built the Taj Mahal as a tomb for his favorite wife. He used the most expensive rocks possible, including white marble and 28 types of precious stone.

Empire State Building ►
Like many modern buildings, the Empire State Building in New York City is faced with limestone and granite. These rocks are attractive, easy to work and polish, yet strong enough to carry great weight.

The pyramids were originally covered in a smooth, shiny white layer of limestone

Mesa Verde ▲
The cliff dwellings at Mesa Verde, Colorado, were built 13 centuries ago from soft sandstone. The builders had to cut the sandstone by hand using stone axes.

Djenné Mosque ▲
The Djenné Mosque in Mali, Africa, is the world's largest mud-brick building. The sun-baked mud bricks were glued together with mud mortar and plastered with more mud.

Start a collection

For most rock hounds, building a collection is the most important part of their hobby. A collection grows better and better over time, and the best specimens can be arranged to make a spectacular display. You can collect rocks, fossils, or minerals, but most people specialize in either fossils or minerals. Whatever you collect, it's important to label all your specimens and keep a careful record of everything you know about them.

WHAT YOU WILL NEED

- Your collection
- White correcting fluid, or white stickers and craft glue
- Black, fine-point permanent marker pen
- 2 index card files
- Specimen trays (see right), matchbox trays, or egg cartons
- Cotton balls or tissue paper
- Magnifying glass

1 **Assemble your specimens**. Put a small dab of correcting fluid on an unimportant part of the bottom of each one and let it dry. Alternatively, use a small white sticker. Stickers will eventually drop off, so you'll need to add extra glue to prevent this from happening. Use the permanent marker pen to write a reference number on each mark or sticker, starting with 1.

Index card file

2 **Fill out an index card** for each specimen, writing its allocated number at the top of the card. Note the type of rock or the name of the mineral or fossil (if you know it) under the number. Also jot down where each specimen came from and any other interesting details. As you learn more about your collection, add the new information to the cards. Keep the cards in numerical order in the file.

Magnifying glass

Correcting fluid

Cotton ball

Put your best specimens in a box and keep them on display in your room

MAKING SPECIMEN TRAYS

You can buy specimen trays from mineral shops, or make your own. Cut out a square or rectangle of posterboard, according to the size of the specimen, and draw on the lines shown on the template below. Ask an adult to score along the lines, then cut out each corner. Fold the scored lines, and tape the corners together, as shown in the pictures on the right.

Score along the lines

Tape

Individual specimen tray template

3 **Prepare a second** index card with the name of the rock, fossil, or mineral at the top and its number under the name. Keep these cards in alphabetical order in a separate card file. You can then look up specimens both by name and by number.

4 **Place each specimen** in a small card tray (see above). Put tissue paper or cotton balls under delicate specimens. Arrange all your specimen trays in a drawer or large box to display them.

Erupting volcano

When volcanoes erupt, molten rock gushes from the ground as lava. Some volcanoes erupt gently, but others explode with a bang, blown open by a blast that can hurl millions of tons of rock debris into the sky. By making a homemade volcano, you can see why eruptions can be so violent.

WHAT YOU WILL NEED

- Small plastic bottle
- Water
- Measuring cup
- Tray or baking sheet
- Sand
- Tablespoon
- Bicarbonate of soda
- Red food coloring
- Dishwashing liquid
- Funnel (if available)
- Vinegar

Sand

Plastic bottle

3 **Pour enough** warm water into the cup to fill the bottle two-thirds full. Add two heaped tablespoons of bicarbonate of soda and stir well. Add a tablespoon each of food coloring and dishwashing liquid to the cup.

2 **Pile up** sand around the bottle to make a volcano shape. Be careful not to let any sand fall down the bottle neck.

1 **Rinse out** a small plastic soda bottle, then use a measuring cup to figure out how much water the bottle holds. Empty the bottle and place it on a tray.

Make your volcano more realistic by placing rocks, plastic trees, or models around it

IMPORTANT

This experiment can be messy, so check with an adult where you should do it. Outdoors on a flat surface, such as a driveway or sidewalk, is a good idea.

4 **Carefully pour** the liquid from the cup into the bottle, using a funnel if you have one. If you don't, pour the liquid very slowly and carefully.

VIOLENT VOLCANOES

Really violent eruptions are caused by gas bubbles, as in the homemade volcano in this activity. When molten rock is trapped underground, high pressure keeps gases dissolved inside it. But if the lava breaks through the surface, the pressure suddenly drops and the gas forms bubbles, pushing up the lava like soda exploding from a bottle.

Ash cloud ▶
Mount Augustine in Alaska erupts, with tons of scalding ash and rubble hurled high into the sky.

5 **Be prepared** for the eruption, which happens very quickly. Measure 1/2 cup of vinegar and pour it into the bottle. Jump back, keeping your eyes on the volcano.

HANDY TIP

If the sand doesn't stick to the bottle, add a little water to it.

On the lava trail

Lava is a bit like molasses. When it's very hot, it becomes thin and runny, but as it cools down, it becomes thicker and stickier. As a result, the temperature of lava, as well as the minerals contained within the lava, affect the way volcanoes grow—as this activity shows.

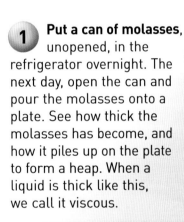

Molasses can from refrigerator

Viscous consistency of cold molasses

1 **Put a can of molasses,** unopened, in the refrigerator overnight. The next day, open the can and pour the molasses onto a plate. See how thick the molasses has become, and how it piles up on the plate to form a heap. When a liquid is thick like this, we call it viscous.

THE COOL THING ABOUT LAVA TUBES

In Hawaii you can walk across flowing lava without burning your feet. The very runny lava from Kilauea Volcano flows for miles in streams, and the surface of a stream sometimes cools and hardens to form a crust. Hot lava carries on flowing beneath the crust, forming a "lava tube" that is insulated by the roof, and so able to flow even further. When the lava finally stops flowing, the tube hardens into a twisting tunnel that people can actually walk through.

Collecting lava ▶
A scientist takes a sample from a lava tube at Kilauea Volcano, Hawaii, one of the world's most active volcanoes. It has been flowing with lava continuously since 1983.

WHAT YOU WILL NEED

- 2 cans of molasses
- 2 plates
- Heatproof bowl or pan
- Boiling water

Ask an adult to pour the boiling water and to put the can in the water.

Smooth, flowing consistency of warmed molasses

Molasses can from pan of hot water

2 **Ask an adult** to do this part of the experiment for you. Boil some water and pour it into a heatproof bowl. Then place the other can of molasses, unopened, in the bowl. Leave the molasses to warm up for half an hour.

3 **Open the can** and pour the warm molasses onto a plate. You'll find that the molasses is much runnier, and spreads quickly to form a wide, flat puddle.

Volcano shapes

The shape of a volcano depends largely on how runny the lava is. Cool lava, or lava containing lots of silica, is very viscous. It builds up into a steep, conical volcano, or a dome volcano. It can also plug a volcano's central vent, causing pressure to build up, and so producing explosive eruptions. Lava that is very hot and contains a lower level of silica minerals tends to be runny. It erupts gently and spreads a long way, building up slowly to form a gently sloping mountain called a shield volcano.

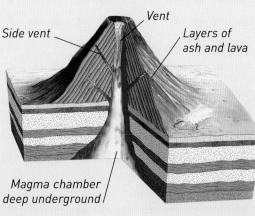

Side vent — *Vent* — *Layers of ash and lava* — *Magma chamber deep underground*

Conical volcano ▲
Conical volcanoes grow from thick, viscous lava, or from ash and rubble that rain down from explosive eruptions. Some are "composite volcanoes," made of alternating layers of both ash and lava.

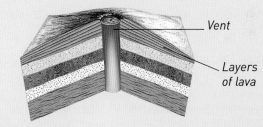

Vent — *Layers of lava*

Shield volcano ▲
Runny lava travels a long way before cooling and solidifying. It builds up into a gently sloping shield volcano. The islands of Hawaii formed this way.

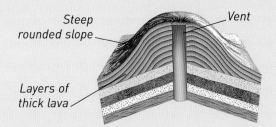

Steep rounded slope — *Vent* — *Layers of thick lava*

Dome volcano ▲
Very viscous lava that cools quickly can barely flow. It grows into a rounded heap, forming a dome volcano. These sometimes form in the craters of volcanoes that have blown apart.

Colored crystals

Crystals are the building blocks of rocks. They form when minerals solidify into regular shapes with flat, often shiny faces and sharp edges. You can find out more about crystals by growing your own from some common household ingredients.

HANDY TIP

To make "amethyst" crystals, mix together blue and red food coloring.

Sugar crystals can take several weeks to grow

1 **Put 3 or 4 tablespoons** of sugar in the measuring cup and pour on about a cup of hot water. Stir until no more sugar will dissolve. If all the sugar dissolves within 1–2 minutes, add another tablespoon. Stir for 2 more minutes. Let the solution cool for 5 minutes.

2 **Meanwhile, tie a paper clip** to a piece of string and wrap the string around the middle of a pencil. Lay the pencil across the top of the jar so that the paper clip is suspended about 1 in (2 cm) above the bottom of the jar.

3 **Lift off the pencil**. Pour sugar solution into the jar until just over three-fourths full. Add 3–4 drops of food coloring. Put the pencil back on the jar. Make a note of the color and the substance dissolved (sugar).

CHEMICAL COLORINGS

The colors of gems often come from chemical impurities, just as your home-grown crystals are colored by additives. Rubies and sapphires are both varieties of the mineral corundum, which is colorless when pure. Rubies get their red from chromium, while sapphires are colored various colors by iron and titanium.

Cross with different-colored sapphires

Salt crystals form on the bottom of the jar as well as on the paper clip

4 **Repeat the above** steps using salt in the second jar, and Epsom salts in the third. Add a different food coloring to the jars so you can tell them apart. Make a note of the color and contents of each jar.

CRYSTALS IN ROCK

Many rocks contain crystals large enough to see. The grains in granite are interlocking crystals of three minerals: mica (black), quartz (gray), and feldspar (pink and white). These crystals grow large because granite forms slowly when molten rock cools underground.

Magnified granite

Epsom salt crystals are long and spiky, and grow very quickly

WHAT YOU WILL NEED

- Tablespoon
- White sugar
- Measuring cup
- Hot water
- 3 paper clips
- String
- 3 pencils
- 3 glass jars
- Food coloring
- Salt
- Epsom salts
- Gloves and goggles

Wear gloves and goggles when using Epsom salts.

Crystal shapes

Crystals have distinctive shapes because of the way atoms line up inside them, and the shape is a useful clue to a mineral's identity. All crystals can be placed in one of six main classes according to their symmetry.

◀ **Cubic** crystals are very symmetrical, which means you keep seeing the same shape if you turn them around. Diamonds are cubic.

Pyrite

◀ **Monoclinic** crystals have much less symmetry than cubic crystals. The shape repeats only once as you turn them around.

Selenite

◀ **Triclinic** crystals are the least symmetrical of all the crystal shapes. They have no equal sides or angles and can look like a jumble of flat faces.

Axinite

◀ **Tetragonal** crystals typically have a rectangular shape, with equal sides and angles. They look a bit like elongated cubes.

Idocrase

◀ **Orthorhombic** crystals are long and have tapered ends, like a rectangle with the corners chipped off. The mineral topaz forms gemstones this shape.

Barite

◀ **Hexagonal** and **trigonal** crystals have six sides. Rubies, sapphires, emeralds, and snowflakes all belong to this class.

Beryl

5 **Check each solution** after 30 minutes to see if crystals are forming. Leave them undisturbed for at least 2 weeks and make a daily check. Do the crystals grow at different speeds or have different shapes?

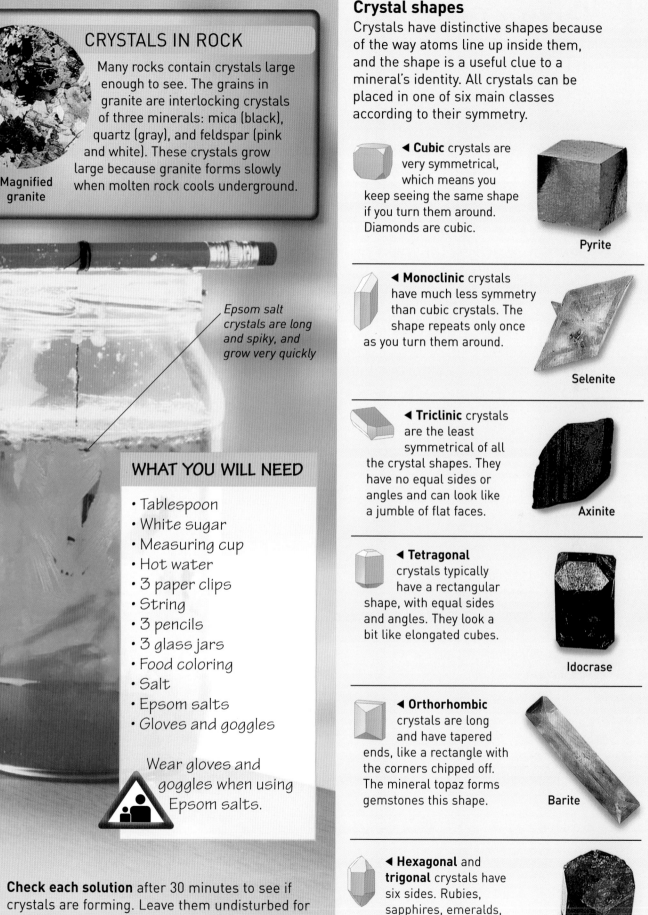

Grow your own gems

In rare conditions, exceptionally beautiful and hard-wearing crystals form in igneous or metamorphic rock to become gemstones. The element carbon can crystallize into a diamond, the most precious jewel of all, and the minerals corundum and beryl can form rubies, sapphires, and emeralds. Gemstones are highly prized for their beauty and rarity. You're unlikely to find any when rock hunting, so why not try making a fake?

IMPORTANT

Wear goggles to protect your eyes from splashes, and wear protective gloves when handling the alum solution. If some of the solution should splash onto your skin, wash it off immediately with lots of cold water. Do not put the alum in your mouth.

WHAT YOU WILL NEED

- Protective goggles
- Protective gloves
- Measuring cup
- Kitchen scale
- Hot water
- Alum (available from toy stores in crystal-growing kits, or from some supermarkets as a pickling salt)
- Mixing stick
- Plate
- Tweezers
- String
- Pencil
- Glass tumbler
- Old saucepan

Ask an adult to supervise the use of alum and to help you heat the alum solution.

ARE DIAMONDS FOREVER?

Diamonds are famous for the way they sparkle. A cut diamond reflects more light than other gems and splits the light into colors, giving the diamond its "fire." They are also famous for being the hardest substance known—no other mineral can scratch them. But they're far from indestructible. Like coal and other forms of carbon, they can burn.

Cut diamonds

The fake gem grows as the alum in the solution crystallizes onto it

1 **Put the empty cup** on the scale and set it to zero. Put on the goggles and gloves. Pour 1¼ cups (300 ml) of hot water into the cup, then add 3½ oz (100 g) of alum. Remove the cup from the scale and stir the solution with the mixing stick until no more alum will dissolve.

2 **Pour a third** of a cup of the solution onto a plate and leave in a warm place to dry. Cover the cup and set it aside. Alum crystals will form quickly on the bottom of the plate as the liquid cools. Let the crystals grow as large as possible. This will take about 2 or 3 hours.

3 **Carefully remove** one of the best crystals with tweezers. Tie a piece of string around it and wrap the string around the middle of a pencil.

4 **Crystals will also have formed** on the bottom of the cup and you will need to redissolve them. Pour the solution into a pan and heat it, then pour it back into the cup and swish it around until all the crystals have dissolved. Let the solution cool for 5 minutes.

HANDY TIP

Add red food coloring to make a ruby, or green to make an emerald.

5 **Pour some of the solution** into the tumbler and hang the crystal tied to the pencil in the solution. Leave the crystal for a few days to grow into a "diamond."

Glittering geodes

In areas where there are porous rocks, you may come across a dull rock shaped like a potato on the ground. These "potato stones" are called geodes and are highly prized by mineral collectors. If the rock is sliced in half, inside is a cavity lined with crystals. You can make a fake geode in a grapefruit skin, using the chemical alum to form the crystals.

WHAT YOU WILL NEED

- Grapefruit or orange
- Aluminum foil
- Plaster of Paris
- Bowl
- Spatula
- Protective goggles
- Protective gloves
- Alum (available in crystal-growing kits or from supermarkets as a pickling salt)
- Hot water
- Measuring cup
- Measuring scale
- Food coloring (optional)

 Ask an adult to supervise the use of alum.

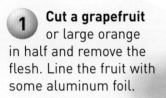

1 **Cut a grapefruit** or large orange in half and remove the flesh. Line the fruit with some aluminum foil.

2 **Mix about a cup** of plaster of Paris powder in a bowl, following the instructions on the package. Leave for 10 minutes, or until it thickens, then spread it over the foil inside the grapefruit with a spatula to form a thick, irregular layer. Before it sets, put on the goggles and gloves, and sprinkle over some alum crystals. Leave for half an hour for the plaster to harden.

3 **Measure about 1¼ cups** (300 ml) of hot water in a jug and add 3½ oz (100 g) of alum. Stir until no more will dissolve. To make an "amethyst" geode, add a teaspoon each of red and blue food coloring. Let cool for 5–10 minutes. Stand the grapefruit in a cup or bowl and fill it with the alum solution. Leave for a few days, topping up with more solution as it evaporates.

HOW GEODES FORM

Geodes form in cavities in porous rock. Fluids rich in dissolved minerals, such as quartz, seep into the cavity. The quartz crystallizes on the inner surface, and the crystals can grow big enough to fill the geode. When the rock erodes, a chunk may break off. The hard crystals hold the chunk together, while the outside wears down to form a dull-looking, potato-shaped rock.

Amethyst geode ▶
This geode is full of amethyst crystals—a purple form of quartz. The crystals are translucent and shaped like pyramids.

4 **After several days**, pour off the solution and peel away the rind and foil to reveal your beautiful "geode"!

You can paint the outside to make it look more like a rock

IMPORTANT

Do not swallow alum. If some should splash onto your skin, wash it off immediately with lots of cold water. Wear goggles to protect your eyes from splashes, and wear protective gloves when handling the alum solution.

How hard is it?

A good way of identifying a mineral is to see how easy it is to scratch. All minerals have a "hardness" rating from 1 to 10 on Mohs scale of hardness (see below), and those with a high number can scratch anything with a lower number on the scale. If you don't have a collection of minerals, you can try out the hardness test using household items.

MOHS SCALE

The German mineralogist Friedrich Mohs developed the hardness scale in 1812. The scale is based on the 10 minerals shown below, starting with talc, which has a hardness of 1. Some everyday equivalents are given alongside the minerals.

Scale	Mineral	Equivalent
1	Talc	Ice = 1.5
2	Gypsum	Fingernail = 2.5
3	Calcite	Penny = 3.5
4	Fluorite	Iron nail = 4.5
5	Apatite	Penknife blade = 5.5
6	Orthoclase	Hard steel file = 6.5
7	Quartz	Sandpaper = 7.5
8	Topaz	Emery board = 8.5
9	Corundum	Ruby = 9
10	Diamond	No equivalent

1 **Put the items** to be scratched in one pile and the scratching tools in another. List the test objects in a notepad.

2 **Try scratching each** test object with your fingernail, which has a hardness of 2.5. Anything it can scratch must have a lower hardness. Make a note of the results.

MINERALS FOR WRITING

Chalk and pencil lead are both good for writing because they contain soft minerals that rub off easily. Oddly, classroom chalk is no longer made from chalk, and pencil lead is not made from lead. Classroom chalk is actually the mineral gypsum, which has a hardness of 2. Pencil lead is the mineral graphite, the hardness of which varies from 1 to 2 (clay is added to make it harder).

"Lead" pencil

Classroom "chalk"

WHAT YOU WILL NEED

- Household objects to scratch: classroom chalk, copper coin, brick, old cutlery, crockery, and glass
- Scratching tools: bronze or copper coin, iron nail, penknife, steel file, and sandpaper
- Notepad and pen

Ask an adult to help you use the penknife, steel file, and sandpaper.

HANDY TIP

Start by making short scratches with the scratching tools and don't apply too much pressure.

3 **Now try scratching** each object with a copper coin. Does it leave a scratch or just a colored streak where the metal has rubbed off on something harder? The coin has a hardness of 3.5, which is low, so most objects are likely to scratch the coin, rather than vice versa. Jot down the results.

4 **Repeat the scratch test** with the iron nail, which has a hardness of 4.5. How easily can the nail scratch the coins? With an adult helping you, try scratching the objects with a penknife blade, a steel file, and sandpaper. Now try to work out the hardness of each test object, then write down your conclusions.

The streak test

A mineral's color can help you identify it, but colors can be misleading. The mineral quartz, for example, comes in many colors. A better way of assessing color is to do a streak test, which always gives the same result. You can look up the streak color of every mineral in a field guide. This test applies only to minerals, not rocks.

WHAT YOU WILL NEED

- Porcelain tiles with white, unglazed backs
- Selection of minerals, such as amethyst, azurite, calcite, chrysocolla, hematite, iron pyrite, limonite, and quartz

Iron pyrite is golden but makes a greenish black streak

Chrysocolla can be green or blue but makes a white streak

COLORS OF QUARTZ

Pure quartz is colorless, but chemical impurities can make it purple (amethyst), pink, green, red, yellow, or black. Quartz is also hard and transparent, so colored forms make good gemstones. But whatever the color, the streak that it makes is always white.

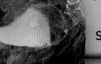

Smoky quartz   Pink quartz

1 **Scratch** the mineral along the back of a tile to make a streak. Keep doing this until the color is clear. Repeat with all the minerals you want to test.

2 **If the mineral** is too hard to make a streak, ask an adult to crush a small amount with a hammer. The color of the streak is really just the color of a mineral's powder.

Calcite can be several colors but always makes a white streak

Amethyst is purple but makes a white streak

Quartz makes a white streak

Limonite varies from yellow to black but makes a yellow-brown streak

Hematite is gray, brown, or black but makes a dark red streak

Azurite leaves a pale blue streak

IMPORTANT

Although the minerals used in this experiment aren't toxic, it is very important that you don't put minerals in your mouth.

LIGHT AND LUSTER

As well as looking at a mineral's color and streak, geologists look at its luster—how it reflects or transmits light, making it shiny or dull. This is also an important clue to a mineral's identity. Some minerals are shiny like metals (metallic luster), others glisten like glass (vitreous or glassy luster), and others are pearly, greasy, or silky. Minerals may be transparent, which means you can see through them; translucent, which means they let light through; or opaque, which means they don't let any light through.

Greasy

Metallic

Calcite produces a double image

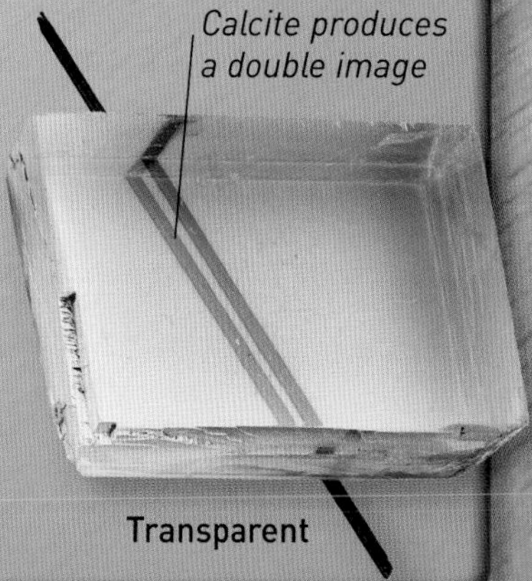

Transparent

Acid test

One of the easiest minerals to identify is calcite—the main ingredient in chalk and limestone. Calcite reacts with liquids that are acidic, such as vinegar. If you drop a rock made of calcite into vinegar, it will fizz and bubble. In this activity, the reaction between calcite and vinegar causes a dramatic color change.

1 **First you need** to prepare the indicator liquid, which shows how acidic a solution is. Boil some red cabbage for about 10 minutes and strain the water into a pitcher. Dilute it until it's transparent but still strongly colored. Pour the diluted cabbage water into the two tumblers.

Pour the diluted cabbage water into glass tumblers

Only a few drops of white vinegar are needed

2 **Now you need** to make the solution acidic. Add a tiny amount of white vinegar, drop by drop, to each tumbler. As soon as the liquid turns pink, stop adding vinegar.

Crush the chalk to a powder to speed up the reaction

WHAT ARE ACIDS?

Acids are chemicals that taste sour (like vinegar) and have certain chemical properties. We measure how acidic a solution is with a dye called an indicator, which changes color. Red cabbage contains a natural indicator that is normally purple but turns pink in acid. When you added chalk to the tumbler, calcite reacted with the acid and "neutralized" it, making the water turn back to purple.

Testing acidity with indicator paper

WHAT YOU WILL NEED

- Small red cabbage, sliced
- Water
- Saucepan
- Pitcher
- Two clean glass tumblers
- White vinegar
- Real chalk or a piece of soft limestone
- Teaspoon

Ask an adult to help you boil the red cabbage.

A pink color shows that the liquid is acidic

A purple or blue color shows that chalk has "neutralized" the acid

3 **Stir a teaspoon** of crushed chalk into one tumbler. Calcite in the chalk reacts with the acid and neutralizes it, turning the solution purple. See if the same reaction happens with other rocks, such as limestone.

CHEMICAL WEATHERING

Rain is naturally slightly acidic because it contains small amounts of the gas carbon dioxide, forming carbonic acid. When rain falls on chalk and limestone, the acid reacts with calcite in the rock and slowly dissolves it. This process, called chemical weathering, can wear away hills and hollow out huge caverns underground.

Guilin Hills, China ▶
These spectacular hills are the remains of a vast block of limestone that was eaten away by rain.

Make paint from minerals

Since the earliest times, people have used colorful minerals to make paint. Unlike paints made from plants and animals, mineral paints hold their color well over time. But they can be difficult to make, especially if the mineral is rock-hard. Soft minerals, like red ocher and chalk, are the simplest to make into paints because they are easy to crush. Harder minerals, like azurite and malachite, are difficult to crush, but they produce brilliant blue and green colors.

WHAT YOU WILL NEED

- Dust mask
- Soft minerals, such as red ocher, chalk, and charcoal
- Mortar and pestle
- 2 shallow bowls
- Egg
- Kitchen towel
- Mixing stick
- Paintbrush and paper

Wear a dust mask when crushing minerals—some may be an inhalation risk.

1 **Wearing a dust mask**, grind a mineral (red ocher here) with a mortar and pestle to make a fine powder. The finer you grind the powder, the smoother the paint will be.

2 **Tip the powder** into a shallow bowl and add a few drops of water. Stir the powder and water together with the pestle until it becomes a smooth paste.

3 **You need to add** a binding agent to the paste to stop it turning to dust when it dries. Egg yolk works well, but it has to be separated from the egg white. Crack open an egg and carefully pour out the white, leaving the yolk in the shell. Roll the yolk very gently in kitchen towel to clean it, then put it in a bowl.

PIGMENTS AND DYES

Pigments and dyes are substances used to create intense colors. Dyes dissolve in water and soak into absorbent materials, such as fabric, coloring them throughout. Pigments work in a different way. They don't dissolve, so they are ground into powder and used to make paint. Most modern pigments and dyes are synthetic.

Azurite, once an important source of blue paint

HANDY TIP

White craft glue can be used as a binding agent instead of egg yolk.

CAVE PAINTINGS

Horse cave painting, Lascaux, France

The finest cave paintings in the world are in Lascaux, western France. About 17,000 years ago, prehistoric painters decorated the walls of the cave with wild animals, mysterious symbols, and monsters that were half human and half animal. The paints that they used were made from ocher, iron oxide, and charcoal.

Dip your paintbrush in water if your paint starts to dry out

Look up cave paintings in books or on the Internet and find one you want to copy

4 **Add a tiny amount** of yolk to the paste—about one-third the amount of paste. Stir it in with a mixing stick. Your paint is now ready to use.

IMPORTANT

If you make paint from very hard minerals, ask an adult to crush them. Don't use any yellow or orange minerals, which can be toxic.

5 **Try making a prehistoric** cave painting with your mineral paints. Use clay or red ocher for the red paint, chalk to make white paint for highlights, and charcoal to make black paint for shadows and outlines.

Here, there, and everywhere

Minerals are everywhere. We use them to build houses and cars, to make computers and TVs, and to wash our clothes, clean our teeth, cook food, and eat with. Even the paper in this book contains at least three of the minerals shown below (talc, clay, and mica). Anything in your home that isn't made from plants and animals is probably made from minerals, but do you know which ones?

Test yourself

Can you guess which of the minerals below are used to make these household objects? Cover the answers, write down your guesses, then check your results. The test is hard, so you may not get many right, but when you know the answers, you can impress your friends with your mineral expertise.

Bauxite

Chromite

Corundum

Fluorite

Graphite

Illite (clay)

Kaolinite (clay)

Magnetite (iron ore)

Mica

Quartz

ANSWERS

1. Ballpoint pen nibs are made of a strong metal called tungsten, which comes from wolframite.

2. Calculators and other electronic gadgets contain microchips made with silicon, the second most common element in Earth's crust. Silicon comes from quartz and many other minerals.

3. Glitter nail polish contains flakes of the shiny mineral mica.

4. Salt is the mineral halite.

5. Terra-cotta pots are made from a clay mineral called illite.

6. Frying pans are made from iron, which comes from hematite and magnetite, or from aluminum, which comes from bauxite. The coating on a nonstick pan is made with the chemical fluorine, from fluorite.

7. Plates and other crockery are made with kaolinite, the main mineral in China clay.

8. Glass is made from the mineral quartz in sand. The sand is melted and mixed with other ingredients before being shaped.

9. Cutlery is usually made of stainless steel, which is a mixture of two metals: iron and chromium. Chromium is added to stop the iron rusting. Iron comes from "iron ores," such as hematite and magnetite; chromium comes from the mineral chromite.

10. Talcum powder is a powdered form of talc, the softest mineral known.

11. Pencil "lead" is not lead but graphite. Clay is added to make the lead harder.

12. Emery boards are good for filing nails because they contain the very hard mineral corundum. Only the mineral diamond is harder than corundum.

13. Incandescent light bulbs contain a fine filament made of the metal tungsten, which comes from wolframite. Tungsten glows when it gets very hot, but it doesn't melt easily.

Halite

Hematite (iron ore)

Talc

Wolframite

Rocks from space

Every day, about 500 tons of dust and rock from space collides with planet Earth. Much of this space debris burns up as it enters the atmosphere, producing streaks of light called shooting stars. However, particles smaller than a millimeter wide can sometimes slip through the air without getting hot enough to burn. These micrometeorites float through the sky as dust, and they fall to the ground in rain. With a powerful magnet—and a bit of luck—you stand a chance of finding one.

WHAT YOU WILL NEED

- Magnet
- Paper cup
- String
- Sheet of white paper
- Magnifying glass
- Tweezers
- Microscope
- Glass slide

1 **Place a powerful magnet** in a paper cup and tie a loop of string to the top of the cup to make a micrometeorite collector. Take the collector outside on a dry day and gently tap it over areas of ground that are dry (but that do get wet after rain) and seldom disturbed by people or vehicles. Good places to try include the ground around downspouts and undisturbed lawns.

2 **When black specks** have appeared on the bottom of the cup, take it indoors and place the cup on some clean white paper. Remove the magnet and tap the cup to shake off the specks.

3 **Use a magnifying** glass and tweezers to pick out particles that look spherical and less than $1/50$ in (half a millimeter) wide. These could be micrometeorites made of iron or nickel, which are magnetic. Particles that are not spherical will be flecks of iron from other sources.

HANDY TIP

Don't touch the dust with the magnet as it will stick to the magnet and be hard to remove.

The loop of string makes a handle

Use the most powerful magnet you have

Place the magnet in the bottom of the cup

WHAT IS A METEORITE?

Artist's impression of a meteorite hitting Earth

Space rocks that land on Earth's surface are called meteorites. Most are fragments of broken asteroids (colossal rocks that orbit the Sun); those made of iron come from the cores of asteroids. Only about 500 meteorites bigger than a football hit Earth each year and most of these end up in the sea.

4 **If you have a microscope**, put the best particles on a glass slide and examine them. Micrometeorites often look smooth because the surface melts as they enter Earth's atmosphere. You can also use a microscope to search for micrometeorites in the dust that appears on cars after rain. This dust comes from high in the sky and contains desert sand and volcanic ash, which may have traveled thousands of miles, as well as micrometeorites.

Iron crystals in micrometeorite

Under the microscope ▸
This is what an iron micrometeorite looks like through a powerful electron microscope. The surface is smooth and round, but crystals of metal are visible.

Glow in the dark

If you shine ultraviolet (UV) light on certain minerals, they glow with extraordinary colors. We call this glow fluorescence. Some minerals always fluoresce with the same color, but others vary according to the impurities they contain. And some minerals continue to glow when you switch off the UV lamp, producing a ghostly light called phosphorescence.

Daylight dullness ▲
All these rocks appear dull in daylight, but they are transforme under a UV lamp (see below).

Fantastic fluorescence

Always follow the manufacturer's instructions and precautions when using a UV lamp, and make sure you have adult supervision. To check minerals for fluorescence, hold them under a long-wave UV lamp in a dark room. Fluorescent minerals are not common, but you can buy them from rock and mineral shops. You can also use a UV lamp to search for fluorescent materials in your home. Paper and fabrics often contain fluorescent brightening agents, and Day-Glo marker pens contain fluorescent dyes. Teeth and fingernails contain the fluorescent mineral apatite. You can also use a UV lamp to hunt spiders and scorpions at night—some species have fluorescent organic chemicals in their skin.

a
Calcite

LET THERE BE LIGHT!

Another way to make rocks glow is to rub them together. Take two pieces of milky quartz into a very dark room and wait 10 minutes for your eyes to adapt. Rub the rocks forcefully and look for an orangey glow—called triboluminescence. Alternatively, crunch on wintergreen-flavored candies in a dark room while looking in a mirror.

Friction produces an orange glow

HANDY TIP

Inexpensive long-wave UV lamps are often sold as "black lights" or disco lights.

WHAT CAUSES FLUORESCENCE?

When ultraviolet light strikes a fluorescent mineral, the atoms in the mineral absorb energy from the light. Tiny particles called electrons, which form the outside of these atoms, become "excited." The electrons then lose the extra energy they have absorbed by emitting particles of visible light, which we see as a colored glow.

Dancing in the dark ▲
Long-wave UV lamps are often used in dance clubs, where they make fluorescent materials, such as glow sticks, emit light in vivid colors.

The long-wave UV lamp causes these minerals to glow in the dark

b
Blue aragonite

c
Opal

d
Sodalite

e
Wernerite

WHAT YOU WILL NEED

- Long-wave UV lamp
- Fluorescent minerals, such as aragonite, calcite, opal, sodalite, and wernerite.

The UV lamp must be bought and used with adult supervision.

Minerals from water

As rain seeps through the ground, it dissolves some of the minerals in rock. Mineral water, seawater, river water, and tap water almost always contain minerals picked up in this way. You can't usually see them, but you can often taste them. In this activity, you can make them visible.

WHAT YOU WILL NEED

Seawater _____

- Four clean, unscratched CD cases, or small squares of completely clear plastic, such as file folders or sandwich bags
- Four different types of water (see step 1)
- Teaspoon

1 **Collect water** from four different sources, such as rainwater, tap water, seawater, and bottled mineral water.

WHERE'S THE WATER GONE?

The salt flats in Death Valley, California, formed in the same way as the cloudy mineral patches on the CD cases in this activity. About 50,000 years ago, Death Valley was a gigantic lake some 90 miles (145 km) long and 600 ft (180 m) deep. When the Ice Age ended, between 14,000 and 10,000 years ago, California became hotter and drier, and the lake dried out completely. Today, all that remains is the parched lake bed, which is covered with a thick crust of mineral salts.

Mineral salts cover Death Valley, once a vast lake

ALL FURRED UP

One of the most common minerals in tap water is calcium bicarbonate, which comes from limestone. Calcium bicarbonate makes water "hard." When hard water boils, heat turns it into calcium carbonate, which is insoluble. This forms most of the furry lime scale you find in electric kettles.

Lime scale on a kettle element

Bottled mineral water

Rainwater

Tap water

2 **Wipe a flat surface**, such as a table or windowsill, clean. Wash your hands thoroughly so that you don't leave greasy fingerprints on the CD cases. Holding the cases by their edges, place them gently on the table, being careful not to scratch them.

3 **Put a teaspoon** of water from each sample in the middle of each CD case so it forms a puddle without spilling over the edge.

4 **Leave the water** to evaporate completely, then hold each CD case up to the light. If there are minerals in the water, you will see cloudy white patches on the case.

Stalactites on string

Stalactites and stalagmites are made of the mineral calcite, which comes from limestone. Since rain is mildly acidic, it dissolves calcite as it seeps through the ground, hollowing out tunnels, potholes, and caves. Dripping water then redeposits the calcite in icicle shapes. With Epsom salts, you can recreate this process in miniature.

HANDY TIP

Don't use nylon or polyester string because it won't absorb the liquid so well.

The string soaks up the Epsom salts solution

1 **Pour the hot water** and Epsom salts into the pitcher. Stir for several minutes until no more Epsom salts dissolve (there should be a residue of Epsom salts at the bottom of the pitcher).

2 **Pour the solution** into the jars. Cut a length of string or yarn, dunk it in a jar, then run it between your fingers to remove any excess liquid. Attach paper clips to each end, and place one in each jar. Position the jars so the string sags in the middle. Place a saucer underneath to catch the drips.

Paper clip attached to end of the string

3 **After an hour**, a drip of liquid— the start of the stalactite— should have formed where the string sags. If the string is completely dry, replace it with a more absorbent type of string or yarn. If the saucer is full of liquid, replace the string with a less absorbent material or remove a little liquid from each jar.

4 **Let the experiment run** for a few days, checking the string daily to see how long the stalactite has become.

WHY DO STALACTITES FORM?

Your Epsom salts stalactite formed because some of the water evaporated as it dripped off the string, causing dissolved Epsom salts to turn back into crystals. A similar thing happens in limestone caves. As cave water drips through air, some of it evaporates. As a result, calcite crystallizes out of the solution and grows into a stalactite.

What's the difference? ▶

The following saying might be useful: StalaC**tites** cling **tight**ly to the Ceiling. StalaG**mites** grow from the Ground and **might** reach the stalactites.

A stalactite grows from the top down

A stalagmite grows from the bottom up

WHAT YOU WILL NEED

- Gloves and goggles
- 2 cups of Epsom salts
- 2 cups of hot water
- Large pitcher
- Mixing stick
- 2 glass jars
- Cotton string or yarn
- 2 paper clips
- Saucer

Wear gloves and goggles when using Epsom salts.

Changing landscape

If you could speed up time, you'd see the rocks on Earth's surface crumbling and washing away, as though they were made of sand. The processes that destroy and carry away rock are called weathering and erosion. When rocks weather, they crumble, rot, and dissolve. The debris is then washed or blown away in the process of erosion. Weathering and erosion usually happen slowly, but they are constantly at work, changing the landscape. You can see evidence of them everywhere.

Weathered tor ▶
The granite "tors" of southern England are slowly being eaten away by weathering. Rain, which is slightly acidic, attacks certain minerals, such as the feldspar in granite. The feldspar turns into clay and washes away. The grains of quartz that are left behind crumble into sand. Dramatic swings in temperature can also weaken rocks, and water can split them when it seeps into crevices and freezes.

Before the land eroded, the top of this butte was at ground level

SMASHING TEST

Some rocks stand up to weathering and erosion much better than others, and this often affects the way landscapes evolve. To see which rocks are toughest, place a selection in a plastic box. If possible, include granite, sandstone, and limestone. Shake the box as violently as you can for 30 seconds, then open the lid and look inside.

◀ Cracking up
Soft rocks like sandstone crumble much more easily than hard rocks like granite. Sandstone may completely disintegrate.

▼ Monument Valley

The flat-topped "buttes" in Monument Valley, Utah, are all that remain of an ancient sandstone landscape that has been worn away by erosion. Flat-topped hills like this can form when a cap of hard rock protects the softer, underlying rock from erosion.

Types of erosion

Water, wind, and ice all contribute to the process of erosion, shifting billions of tons of rock debris every year and carrying it relentlessly downhill. Much of the debris ends up dumped in floodplains, deltas, or the sea.

River ▶
Rock debris, in the form of sand, silt, and clay, is transported long distances by rivers. The gritty water also eats away at the surroundings, creating valleys.

Sea ▶
Pounding waves erode the coast, undercutting cliffs and making them collapse. As the coast retreats, crumbling arches and towers of rock are left behind.

Wind ▶
The wind erodes the land in deserts. It picks up fine dust and carries it far away. Sand is blasted against rocks, sculpting them into weird and wonderful shapes.

Earth ▶
Landslides happen when unstable heaps of eroded rubble and earth suddenly collapse. They are often triggered by earthquakes or torrential rain.

Ice ▶
Glaciers pick up rock rubble as they slide slowly forward. The rubble scrapes the land, carving out valleys.

Freeze and thaw

Given enough time, water can alter or destroy rocks, including the very hardest ones. One way that water attacks rocks is through the action of ice. Liquid water seeps into pores and crevices in rock, and then freezes when the temperature drops. As the water freezes, it expands, exerting enough pressure to split the rock into chunks. With this activity, you can see the "freeze–thaw" process for yourself.

WHAT YOU WILL NEED

- 10 different rocks, including several sedimentary rocks such as sandstone, limestone, clay, or chalk
- Plastic sandwich box
- Notepad
- Pen
- Water

As the rock's surface breaks down, water seeps deeper into it

1 **Arrange 10 different rocks** in the bottom of a plastic sandwich box. Sketch the arrangement in a notepad so you can remember which rock is which. Note the names of the rocks, if you know them, or write a brief description, such as "hard, shiny, and pink." Cover the rocks with water, seal the lid, and place the box in the freezer.

2 **Leave the box** in the freezer overnight so that the water freezes completely. Take the box out of the freezer and place it in the sink while the ice thaws. Once the ice has turned to water, remove the lid. Look at the rocks and gently touch them with your fingers. Have any broken or started to crumble?

WEIGHT-LIFTING ICE

Fill a strong glass bowl with water, then rest a saucer on top. Place a heavy weight (up to 9 lb/4 kg) on the saucer, and put it in the freezer for 24 hours. When you remove it from the freezer, you will see that the ice has lifted the saucer and weight off the bowl.

Expanding ice lifts the saucer and weight

HANDY TIP

Make the ice out of boiled water—it will be less cloudy.

THE DESTRUCTIVE POWER OF ICE

In spring, snow melts during the day but freezes again at night

Scree litters the bottom of the mountain

Scree at Wheeler Peak, Nevada

A good place to see the weathering power of ice is on mountains. In these cold, wet places, water often freezes at night but thaws in the morning. The endless cycle of freezing and thawing slowly but steadily eats away at the rock, making it crumble into piles of rubble called scree. These fragments have a greater surface area, making the weathering process work even faster. Over time and in certain conditions, the power of ice and water can wear whole mountains down to nothing.

Softer rocks appear crumbly

Each time the water freezes, ice crystals attack the rock

3 **Replace the lid** on the box and put the box back in the freezer, adding more water to the box, if necessary, to cover the rocks. Freeze and thaw the rocks at least five more times, and over several days.

4 **Pour out the water** and let the rocks dry before inspecting them. Count them and compare them to your sketch to see which have changed the most. Sandstone will have a soft, crumbly surface, and chalk may have broken apart. Sedimentary rocks will have softened the most, and igneous rocks, such as granite, will probably be unaffected. Porous rocks, which contain lots of tiny holes, weather most quickly because water can seep into them easily.

Ice Age spotter

For much of the past 2 million years, Earth was in the grip of a freezing period called the Ice Age. Sheets of ice 1.5 miles (2.4 km) thick stretched from the North Pole to beyond the Great Lakes. Canada and much of northwest Europe disappeared under an ice sheet bigger than Antarctica. The ice melted 14–10,000 years ago, but it left its mark all over the landscapes of North America and Europe.

Glacial valleys are usually broad with steep sides, forming a "U" shape

SLOW-FLOWING RIVERS OF ICE

A glacier is a river of ice that flows extremely slowly, by a few inches a day at most. Its source is high on a mountain, where snow builds up annually and compresses underlying layers into ice. The ice flows downhill, scraping the land with tremendous force and tearing boulders off the ground. Rubble sticks to the bottom of a glacier, forming an abrasive surface that makes the ice even more destructive.

◀ **Hubbard Glacier**
Glaciers are still at work in many places. This glacier in Alaska, with its 300-ft- (90-m-) high terminal wall, flows to the sea, where it breaks up into icebergs.

Yosemite Valley

A good place to spot Ice Age features is Yosemite Valley, California. The broad, steep-sided valley was carved out of solid granite by a massive glacier. Smaller, adjoining glaciers carved out shallower, U-shaped valleys that often have waterfalls where they meet the main valley. These are called hanging valleys.

Hanging valley

Ice Age features

If you live in North America or Europe, look out for Ice Age features next time you go out in the country. Some of the features below are very common, especially in hilly areas. You can see similar features in places that still have glaciers, like high mountains.

◄ Arête
An arête is a steep-sided, sharp-edged ridge formed between two glaciers that carved neighboring valleys. Hiking on an arête gives sweeping views.

Cirque ►
A cirque is a rounded basin found high in hills, carved out long ago by the mass of ice at the source of a glacier. Often, a cirque fills with water, forming a lake called a tarn.

◄ Erratic
An erratic is an enormous boulder that has been carried by glaciers, and eventually dumped far away from its place of origin after the ice has melted.

◄ Horn
A horn is a pyramid-shaped mountain peak, created by several glaciers eroding different sides of the same mountain. The Matterhorn in Switzerland is a famous example of a glacial horn.

Polished pebbles

Rock tumblers can turn drab lumps of rock into beautiful shiny pebbles and semiprecious stones. Professional rock tumblers are expensive, but many toy stores stock small, inexpensive tumblers that do just the same job and come with a selection of rocks to get you started. Once you've mastered the technique, try polishing rocks you've collected yourself. The results are often surprising and sometimes spectacular.

WHAT YOU WILL NEED

- Coarse rocks
- Rock tumbler
- Grinding grit (coarse, medium, and fine)
- Polishing grit
- Water
- Sieve or colander
- Scrub brush

Check the rock tumbler's instruction manual for the type and number of rocks to use, and how long you should tumble them for.

The rocks look dull and rough before tumbling

Coarse grit

NATURAL ROCK TUMBLERS

Next time you visit a river, look out for smooth, shiny pebbles. Just like the stones in the rock tumbler in this activity, pebbles form when rocks are worn down by tumbling in gritty water. It takes thousands of years for pebbles to form naturally, and only the toughest minerals survive. As a result, rivers are a good place to look for hard minerals such as quartz and gemstones.

◄ **White water**
Rocks are eventually worn into smooth, shiny pebbles in fast-moving water, such as this mountain stream.

1 **Choose the rocks** you want to polish. Make sure they are suitable for your rock tumbler by checking the instruction manual.

2 **Wash the rocks** thoroughly and place them in the tumbler. Add the coarse grinding grit and water, according to the manual, and switch on the tumbler. Depending on how rough the rocks are, this stage may take up to a week.

This rock tumbler has timer buttons that stop the machine after a preset period

HANDY TIP

Rocks with interesting colors or patterns look the best when polished.

After the first tumble, the rocks look round and smooth

The rocks are shiny after the final tumble in polishing grit

Fine grit

Polishing grit

3 **Stop the tumbler** and tip the contents into a sieve. Rinse away the grit with plenty of fresh water. Clean the inside of the drum thoroughly with a damp cloth. Put the washed rocks back in the tumbler with medium grit and water, and tumble for about 4–7 days (or as long as the instruction manual says).

4 **Stop the tumbler**, wash everything thoroughly, and repeat the process with fine grit. After tumbling, clean the rocks and tumbler even more thoroughly than before so that the rocks won't get scratched in the final stage. Use a scrub brush to clean them, and make sure the tumbler is spotless.

5 **Put the rocks** back in the tumbler with the final polishing grit and tumble again according to the manual.

Plant power

If you've ever seen buckled and cracked pavement around a tree, you'll know that plant roots can exert tremendous forces on their surroundings. These forces can break down rock, speeding up the process of weathering. You can recreate the effect in miniature by growing broad bean seedlings in a cup of plaster of Paris.

WHAT YOU WILL NEED

- Mixing stick, such as a lollipop stick
- Plaster of Paris
- Plastic cup
- Broad beans

1 **With a mixing stick**, make up enough plaster of Paris (following the instructions on the package) to fill the plastic cup about two-thirds full. Add the mixture to the cup.

Mixing stick

Plaster of Paris visible through plastic cup

BIOLOGICAL WEATHERING

Living things contribute to the process of weathering in lots of ways. Bacteria and algae flourish in damp rock crevices, and lichens can grow across bare rock. All these organisms make the rock surface damp and acidic. The water and acid attack minerals, weakening the rock. Seeds that germinate in rock crevices expand as they draw in water, just as the broad beans did in this activity. The force of this expansion can be powerful enough to split the rock, especially if it has already started to weather. Burrowing animals, like the hamster below, also help speed up the weathering process. As they tunnel through the ground, they not only break up soft rock but also stir the fragments into the soil.

◄ Roots through rock
Tree roots can work their way into crevices in soft rock. When the roots grow and expand, they can eventually break the rock apart.

WHERE DOES SOIL COME FROM?

When rock weathers and crumbles, the particles build up on the ground and mix with rotting organic matter to form soil.

The type of rock in soil affects its characteristics. Soil containing lots of clay is sticky and holds water well, but soil with lots of sand or chalk is crumbly and lets water through. Soil speeds up the process of weathering by trapping water and acids that attack minerals in rock.

Clay

Chalk

Broad bean plant growing in plaster of Paris

2 **When the plaster** of Paris has thickened but not set, push three or four broad beans into it. Make sure the top quarter of each bean is visible above the surface of the plaster.

3 **Watch the beans** for at least a week. The beans will start to germinate and their roots will crack the plaster. When the plants have grown some leaves, remove the plaster from the cup and take a closer look.

Roots penetrate the plaster of Paris

HANDY TIP

Add a teaspoon of water to the cup each day so the seedlings don't dry out and die.

Sandstone sand castles

Sandstone is a common type of sedimentary rock. It forms when buried sand slowly solidifies as minerals crystallize between the sand grains, gluing them together. You can recreate this process with sand, water, and a range of different binding agents.

WHAT YOU WILL NEED

- 6 plastic cups
- Sand
- 5 clear plastic bags
- Tablespoon
- Salt
- Water
- Newspaper
- Tray
- Marker pen
- Plaster of Paris powder
- Corn starch
- Garden soil
- Pitcher of water

Salt plus sand

Plaster of Paris plus sand

THE SAND CYCLE

Sand comes from rocks that have been slowly broken down (weathered) by rain, ice, heat, and other forces. Many minerals in the rocks break down into clay, but quartz, which is very tough, survives as sand grains. Rivers wash these away and dump them in seas and lakes, where they build up in layers. Over long periods, water trickling through the layers deposits minerals such as silica and calcite, which crystallize and "cement" the grains together. And so the sand turns back into new rock: sandstone.

The sands of time ▼
As rocks weather over thousands of years, they crumble into smaller and smaller particles. Eventually, only tiny grains of sand are left.

ROCK BANDS

Sedimentary rocks form layer by layer as debris settles on the floor of a lake or sea, or as windblown sand or dust settles on the ground. When the rocks are exposed again at the surface, millions of years later, the layers are often visible as bands, or "strata," with the youngest strata closest to the top. Geologists can work out the relative age of the strata by identifying any fossils in them.

Vermilion Cliffs in Arizona formed from desert sand dunes

IMPORTANT

As this activity can be very messy, especially the final step, it is best to do it outdoors.

Corn starch plus sand

Soil plus sand

Sand on its own

1 **Almost fill** a plastic cup with sand and empty it into one of the bags. Add 2–3 tablespoons of salt. Shake the bag. Add 4–5 tablespoons of water. Mix the contents by squeezing the bag until the mixture is wet enough to form a sand castle.

2 **Fill a plastic cup** with the mixture and press down on the top to make it even. Place a thick layer of newspaper on a tray and tip out the sand to form a sand castle. Label it "Salt plus sand."

3 **Repeat these steps** to make three more sand castles, but instead of adding salt to the sand, use plaster of Paris, corn starch, and then soil. Crumble the soil well with your hands and remove any stones. Finally, make a fifth sand castle with just sand and water.

4 **Leave the tray** somewhere dry until the sand castles dry out completely and harden. Touch them carefully with your fingers. The plaster of Paris castle will feel the most solid, while the sand-and-water castle will feel the most fragile.

5 **Place the tray** carefully on the ground. Fill a pitcher with water and gently pour about the same amount of water over each sand castle. Which ones wash away most easily? Which is the toughest? When you know the answer, why not make a long-lasting sand sculpture?

Fossil spotter

If you go hunting for fossils, it helps to know what to look for. The most common fossils are not bones of land animals like dinosaurs, but the remains of small sea creatures. Sea animals fossilize more easily because the muddy sea floor can preserve them. Usually only the hardest body parts survive, such as shells, teeth, and bones.

▲ Brachiopod
Most fossils with two hinged shells are bivalves or brachiopods. Both sides of a brachiopod's shell are symmetrical; bivalves have left and right shells that are mirror images.

◄ Belemnite
Bullet-shaped fossils are the internal shells of animals called belemnites, which were very much like modern squid. Like squid, they had long, torpedo-shaped bodies, ten arms, and an ink sac.

Ammonites were very common during the age of the dinosaurs

◄ Ammonite
These sea animals look a little like snails, but were in fact fast-swimming predators. Their shells were divided into compartments, with the animal in the largest, outer compartment. As the animal grew, it added new compartments, forming a spiral. The largest ammonites grew to 6 ft (2 m) wide.

▲ Fish fossil

It's rare to find a whole fossil fish, but fossilized teeth—especially shark teeth—are very common. This fossil is of a bony fish that lived about 50 million years ago. Our backbones first evolved in a group of primitive fish over 500 million years ago.

Crinoids used feathery arms to trap tiny sea creatures drifting through the water

▲ Crinoid

Crinoids, or sea lilies, look like flowers, but they are animals related to starfish. They still exist but were more common in the past. They anchor themselves to the sea floor by a long stalk.

Armor-plated bodies protected trilobites from attack

◄ Trilobite

Trilobites scuttled around on the sea floor like lobsters 590–250 million years ago. Their fossils are common because they molted as they grew. Many had large eyes made of transparent crystals of the mineral calcite.

How fossils form

Special circumstances are needed for fossils to form. As a result, only a tiny fraction of the prehistoric animals that lived on Earth became fossilized (and only a tiny fraction of those have been found). The pictures below show how a fish might become fossilized on the sea floor.

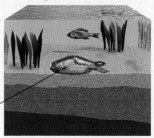

The dead fish settles in mud on the sea floor

▲ Death

The fish dies and sinks to the sea floor. Worms and microbes eat the soft parts of its body as it sinks into the mud.

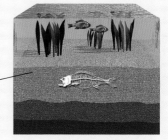

A layer of slimy mud buries the skeleton and helps preserve it

▲ Burial

Silt and sand build up over the skeleton, burying it. Deep in the mud there is less oxygen, so the decaying process slows down.

New layers of sediment build up on top

The mud is compressed into rock

▲ Rock formation

Over thousands of years, the mud turns into rock, such as shale or limestone. The skeleton is slowly replaced by minerals and turns into rock.

Fossil becomes visible as the rock erodes

▲ Discovery

Millions of years later, movements in Earth's crust have brought the rock to the surface of the land, where the fossil may be discovered.

Hunt for fossils

Hunting for fossils is a great hobby. Provided you choose the right site, fossils are surprisingly easy to find. To find a good site in your area, check the Internet or contact a local museum. The best sites are often places where sedimentary rocks are eroding rapidly, such as beaches, cliffs, and quarries. These sites can be dangerous, so be sure to follow the safety precautions on pages 8–9.

Fossil fern
Look for interesting patterns in the rock, such as this fossil fern in sandstone. You can also find good fossils in limestone, clay, and chalk.

IMPORTANT

Some fossil sites are private or protected by law. Don't enter the site without permission. Don't collect or keep fossils until you've checked the rules for the site.

1 Depending on the site you choose, you might find fossils by walking slowly and scanning the ground, by cracking open soft rocks, or by scraping mud. Excellent fossils are often found lying among gravel.

2 Wrap your fossils carefully in paper or cloth to protect them and put them in a bag. Jot down where you found each fossil. When you get home, clean the fossils gently with a toothbrush. Remove any stubborn grit with a penknife. Soak fossils from a beach in cold water to remove salt. Broken fossils can be mended with craft glue; fragile fossils can be painted with diluted craft glue to seal the surface.

This sea snail lived 300 million years ago

Field guides help you identify fossils

WHAT YOU WILL NEED

- Paper or cloth for wrapping fossils
- Notepad and pen
- Shoulder bag
- Toothbrush
- Bucket of water
- Highly visible clothing
- Sturdy boots

Make sure you are accompanied by an adult and follow the code of conduct on page 11.

VISITING MUSEUMS

A good way to find out about the fossils in your area is to visit a natural history museum. Large museums don't just have dinosaur skeletons—they also have dozens of small fossils of the kind you're likely to find on beaches or in quarries. Museum exhibits may show you what the animals used to look like, how they lived, and the kind of environment they inhabited. Museum staff may help you identify your fossils and will tell you if they're valuable.

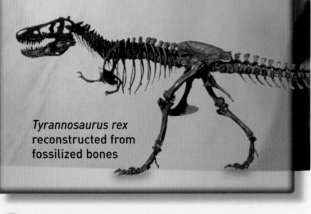

Tyrannosaurus rex reconstructed from fossilized bones

3 **To identify your fossil,** look in a field guide or take it to a local museum. You need to keep a record of where you found the fossil because the location is an important clue to the age of the fossil and its identity, which makes it more valuable.

Geological timescale

Sedimentary rocks are laid down in strata (layers), with younger strata on top of older ones. By studying sedimentary rocks over the world, geologists have identified a sequence of major strata, each containing a distinctive group of fossils. The names of these strata correspond to major periods in Earth's history. Together they form what scientists call the geological column.

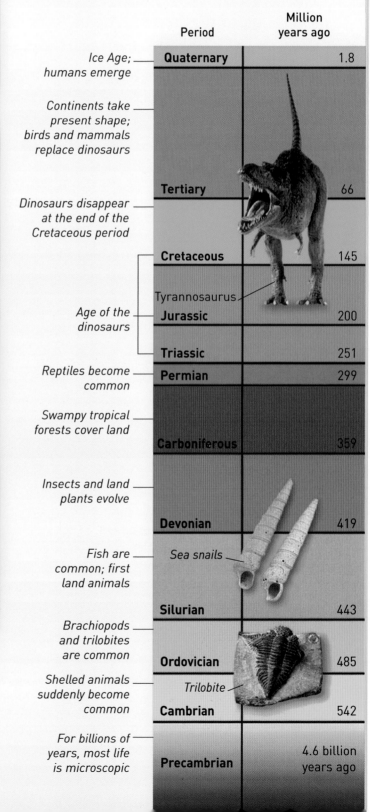

Period	Million years ago
Quaternary	1.8
Tertiary	66
Cretaceous	145
Jurassic	200
Triassic	251
Permian	299
Carboniferous	359
Devonian	419
Silurian	443
Ordovician	485
Cambrian	542
Precambrian	4.6 billion years ago

Ice Age; humans emerge

Continents take present shape; birds and mammals replace dinosaurs

Dinosaurs disappear at the end of the Cretaceous period

Tyrannosaurus

Age of the dinosaurs

Reptiles become common

Swampy tropical forests cover land

Insects and land plants evolve

Fish are common; first land animals — *Sea snails*

Brachiopods and trilobites are common

Shelled animals suddenly become common — *Trilobite*

For billions of years, most life is microscopic

Fake fossils

Most fossils are not ancient, hardened bodies but mineral replicas. They normally take millions of years to form, but you can make your own rocky replica in just a day from plaster of Paris. Use this technique to make copies of real fossils, or to "fossilize" anything from plastic toys to your own hand print.

WHAT YOU WILL NEED

- Plasticine or modeling clay
- Rolling pin
- Petroleum jelly
- Objects to "fossilize," such as seashells, plastic toys, or a real fossil, such as an ammonite
- Heavy paper
- Plaster of Paris
- Water
- Small plastic container

Fossilized seashell

Fake pterodactyl fossil

HANDY TIP

If you use modeling clay for your mold, keep it and let it harden to make an "imprint" fossil.

1 **Knead a large piece** of Plasticine until it becomes soft and easy to shape, then make a thick, round shape out of it. Flatten the top with a rolling pin and smear petroleum jelly over the top.

2 **Press the object** you want to "fossilize" into the Plasticine. (If you use a real fossil, wrap it in plastic wrap to stop it from picking up petroleum jelly or Plasticine.) Remove the object from the Plasticine, taking care not to damage the mold. The mold is now ready to use.

IMPRESSIVE FOSSILS

Many fossils form in exactly the same way as you made your fake fossils with a mold and cast—as impressions in clay, mud, or other soft sediments. The impression fills up with a different kind of sediment, gets buried, and hardens over time to form rock. Fossil impressions can preserve all sorts of structures, from dinosaur footprints to delicate leaves and the feathers of the very first bird.

Fossilized leaves ▶
This fossilized impression of a horsetail plant was formed around 300 million years ago.

Copy of an ammonite fossil

Plaster of Paris

Paper to contain plaster of Paris

3 **Cut out a strip** of paper about 2 in (5 cm) wide and 12 in (30 cm) long. Gently push it partway into the Plasticine to form a circle around the mold.

4 **Mix the plaster of Paris** with water, following the instructions on the packet, in the container. Add yellow food coloring for a sandy color, or black ink to make it gray. For a gritty texture, add sand.

5 **Wait for the plaster** to thicken, then pour it into the mold. Leave for a day to set, then carefully remove your fossil. To make the fossil look more realistic, paint it a slightly different color from the base. Chip the edges off the base so that it looks more like a real rock.

Make a fossil bone

Bone, wood, and other organic substances are porous, which means they're riddled with tiny holes. When porous substances fossilize, water seeps into them, depositing mineral crystals. Watch this process yourself by "fossilizing" a bath sponge.

HANDY TIP

If the sponge doesn't soak up the liquid, put on some protective gloves and give it a squeeze.

WHAT YOU WILL NEED

- Synthetic bath sponge
- Felt-tip pen
- Scissors
- Protective gloves and goggles
- Epsom salts
- Measuring cup
- Hot water
- Mixing stick
- Plastic container
- Magnifying glass

⚠ Wear gloves and goggles when using Epsom salts.

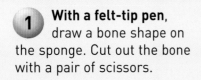

Bone outline made with felt-tip pen

1 **With a felt-tip pen**, draw a bone shape on the sponge. Cut out the bone with a pair of scissors.

2 **Pour about a cup** of hot water into a large measuring cup, then add about 2/3 of a cup of Epsom salts to the cup. Stir until no more salts will dissolve. If you like, add a few drops of food coloring so that you can see the solution soak into the sponge bone.

3 **Place the bone** in a plastic container and pour in some Epsom salts solution, until about one-third of the bone is covered. The sponge should start to soak up the solution.

The Epsom salts solution soaks through the sponge

FROM TREES TO ROCKS

Some 225 million years ago, the state of Arizona was a land of giant conifer trees, dinosaurs, and other reptiles. Remnants of the mighty forest still litter the ground at Petrified Forest National Park, where trees were toppled by a great flood, and buried under vast piles of silt that slowed their decay. Over millennia, water trickling through the ground "petrified" the wood, replacing it completely with multicolored quartz crystals.

Petrified Forest National Park, Arizona

Crystals form in the small holes in the sponge and on its surface

ANCIENT BONES

The fossilized bones of dinosaurs and other prehistoric beasts are not really bones at all—over time, most bones are completely replaced by rock. The soft parts of a dead animal rot away first, leaving the hard parts like bones, teeth, and claws. These are porous just like your sponge, which means water can seep into them. Eventually, water trickling through the ground dissolves the bone and deposits other minerals in its place, such as silica, calcite, or pyrite. These minerals form a rock—a replica of the original animal, which is then said to be "mineralized," or "petrified."

4 **Leave the sponge** for a few days, turning it daily. When the solution has nearly dried out, pick up the bone. It should feel heavier and harder. Look at the crystals that have formed with a magnifying glass.

Eryops, an amphibian living 286 million years ago

Fake shelly limestone

Some types of limestone are made almost entirely of fossils. Often the fossils are too small or fragmented to recognize, but in shelly limestone they are very clear. If you split open a shelly limestone, you'll find beautifully preserved seashells that have been hidden for millions of years. With a bit of cunning, you can make convincing fake shelly limestone.

The plaster sets to form a "matrix" around the shells

WHAT YOU WILL NEED

- Seashells
- Plaster of Paris
- Plastic container
- Plasticine or modeling clay
- Mallet or hammer
- Chisel

Ask an adult to use the mallet and chisel for you.

1 **Collect a variety** of seashells from a beach. Break up some of them into smaller pieces.

2 **Mix the plaster of Paris** with water, following the instructions on the package, in the plastic container. Stir in your shells. For white limestone, leave it as it is. For a sandy color, make the plaster with cold black coffee, or add yellow food coloring. Add sand to make it feel gritty. Make a rough-shaped mold with Plasticine and pour in your mixture.

Plaster of Paris mixed with shells

HOW CHALK FORMS

Chalk is a type of limestone made from microscopic fossils. The fossils usually come from tiny algae called coccolithophores, which float in the sea. Their shells are made of overlapping plates (coccoliths). When coccolithophores die, their shells drop to the sea floor and fall apart. Over millions of years, they build up and are compressed to form chalk.

White chalk cliffs ▶
The chalk in the towering cliffs of the English south coast consists mostly of coccolith fossils that fell to the sea floor more than 65 million years ago.

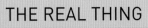

Coccolithophore shell magnified

THE REAL THING

Shelly limestone, which forms on the floor of tropical seas, is made from the shells and body parts of dead sea animals. The most common shells are from animals called bivalves and brachiopods, but you can also find snail shells and ammonites. Other types of limestone are made of fossil corals, or the stalks of elegant animals called crinoids (sea lilies). In Bermuda, people build houses from a local shelly limestone called coquina, and you can see hundreds of fossils embedded in the walls.

Freshwater snails

Brachiopod shells

Sea snails

3 **Let the plaster** harden overnight. "Demold" your fake limestone and ask an adult to split it open with a mallet, or hammer and chisel. Inspect the small bits of shell and pebble embedded in the rock.

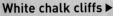

Hit the chisel very gently—the plaster will break easily

Trapped in amber

The most perfect fossils of all form when animals get trapped in pine resin—the sticky gum that oozes from wounded trees. Pine resin forms an airtight seal that preserves an animal's body. Over thousands of years, the resin turns into a hard golden material called amber. With modeling resin, you can make an "amber" fossil of an insect overnight.

Trapped insect in real amber

WHAT YOU WILL NEED

- Dead insects
- Plasticine or modeling clay
- Pebble
- Petroleum jelly
- Protective gloves
- Clear modeling resin (available from art supply stores)
- Yellow food coloring or turmeric
- Cocktail stick

Modeling resin must be handled with great care and not ingested. Ask an adult to mix the resin.

Mold created with a pebble

1. **Collect a few dead insects** and choose the most intact specimen. Good places to look for dead insects are cobwebs and indoor windowsills.

2. **Create a pebble-shaped mold** with Plasticine or modeling clay. Do this by pushing a smooth pebble into the clay, pulling it out, and then widening the bottom of the cavity with a finger. Take care to keep the inner surface of the cavity smooth. Line the inside of the mold with a little petroleum jelly.

3. **Get an adult** to mix the modeling resin, following the manufacturer's instructions carefully, and wearing protective gloves. Usually there are two parts to the mixture—the resin and a hardener—which need to be combined.

4. **To color the resin** yellow, add a tiny drop of yellow food coloring, or a very, very tiny pinch of turmeric. Turmeric will give a slightly less clear "amber."

HANDY TIP

If the insect is fragile, half-fill the mold with resin, put in the insect, then fill to the top.

Almost fill the mold with resin

BRINGING BACK THE DINOSAURS

In the film *Jurassic Park*, a scientist extracts dinosaur DNA from a mosquito in amber and brings dinosaurs back to life. This could never happen in reality because DNA disintegrates in fossils. Other body parts, however, are superbly preserved in amber. Insects 100 million years old look as if they died only yesterday, and their tiny mouthparts and wings appear intact under a microscope. Even small lizards and frogs have been preserved in amber. Thanks to amber fossils, scientists know that bees, ants, flies, and all the other main types of insect were present on Earth 100 million years ago.

Hatching dinosaurs (a scene from *Jurassic Park*)

This ant will stay preserved for years

The top surface of the resin is clearest

5 **Pour the resin** into the mold, taking care not to overfill it. Drop the insect on the surface and push it down very gently into the resin with a cocktail stick.

6 **After 24 hours** (or when the manufacturer's instructions say that the resin is solid), remove the amber stone from the mold and wash it with soapy water.

Amber jewelry
You can turn your amber fossil into a necklace or keyring. Ask an adult to drill a small hole through the fossil so that you can attach a chain to it.

Fossil mud pie

Professional fossil hunters (paleontologists) spend weeks at a time digging through soil, sand, and rock for fossils. To protect the fossils, they scrape away the soil very gently, removing it layer by layer. To find out how to dig for fossils, make a fossil mud pie. This is more fun if you do it with a friend and swap mud pies. But don't let your friend see what you hide in yours!

WHAT YOU WILL NEED

- Objects to bury (see step 1 for examples)
- Garden soil (clay-rich soil works best)
- Garden spade
- Bucket
- Mug
- Old mixing bowl or large plastic container
- Water
- Trowel or screwdriver
- Paintbrush
- Toothpick
- Tweezers

An adult may need to help you dig up the soil.

This mud pie is flat, but yours can be any shape

Excavate your fossils slowly and carefully, working from the edge of the mud pie

1 **Search your home** or garden for hard, dead objects that might make fossils in the future, such as bones, shells, seeds, and pebbles. Include a few "human artifacts" as well, such as coins, marbles, and small plastic models.

2 **Collect three** or four spadefuls of soil in a bucket. Ask an adult to break up the soil with the spade, then use your hands to crumble it as finely as possible. Remove any stones or bits of wood, and break up any lumps of soft clay with your fingers.

3 **Transfer about six** mugs of the broken-up soil to an old mixing bowl or plastic container. Add half a cup of water and mix with your hands to form a very thick mud. Add more water as necessary until the mud is thick enough to form into a solid lump, but isn't runny.

4 **Mold the mud** into a large clod and bury your "fossils" inside it. Leave it to set in the bowl or container in a dry place for a few days.

HANDY TIP

If your soil is very crumbly or sandy, add flour and water to make it stickier.

5 **Once your** fossil mud pie has set, swap it with your friend's. Carefully excavate the fossils with a trowel or screwdriver, brushing the soil away gently with a paintbrush. If you find a small delicate item, use a toothpick or tweezers to remove it gently from the pie.

IMPORTANT

Check with an adult that the mug and mixing bowl you use for the experiment are not still used for drinks and food. It's best to do this experiment outdoors—it could be messy.

RECONSTRUCTING THE PAST

Digging for fossils is only one part of a paleontologist's job. When a skeleton has been excavated, the paleontologist must put together the pieces of the skeleton like a jigsaw puzzle. The bones are analyzed for any signs of disease or injury, and the rock around the bones is searched for clues about when and where the animal or person lived, and the probable cause of death.

Fossil rhinoceros ▶
Paleontologists excavate a 10-million-year-old rhino in Nebraska. It was killed by a cloud of volcanic ash, which hardened around the body, preserving it.

Glossary

Alum A salt that is sometimes used as a fixative in dyeing. Its chemical name is potassium aluminium sulphate.

Arête A narrow mountain ridge formed between two glacial valleys or cirques.

Basalt The most common type of volcanic rock, formed as lava cools and hardens.

Bedrock The layer of rock underneath loose material such as soil or sand.

Calcite The main mineral in limestone and chalk. Its chemical name is calcium carbonate.

Cirque A steep-sided, bowl-shaped hollow in a mountain, carved out by a glacier.

Clay Mineral particles that are smaller than about 0.00008 in (0.002 mm) wide, and are common in soil and sediment. Clay forms by the weathering of granite and other rocks.

Crust The outer layer of Earth that lies over the mantle. There are two main types of crust: continental and oceanic.

Crystal A geometric form of a mineral or other solid, with naturally formed plane faces that reflect the arrangement of the atoms that make it up.

Deposit To lay down a material such as sand, mud, or gravel in a new location.

Desert An arid region that typically receives less than 10 in (250 mm) of rain a year.

Dinosaur A member of a prehistoric family of reptiles that lived from 230 million years ago up to 65 million years ago. Their closest living relatives include birds and crocodiles.

Erosion The wearing away and removal of exposed land by water, wind, and ice.

Erratic A large rock that has been carried by a glacier and dropped far from its place of origin.

Fossil The remains, traces, or impressions of organisms, such as plants and animals, that lived millions of years ago.

Geode A stone containing a crystal-lined cavity.

Glacier A large mass of ice that forms on land and flows slowly downhill under its own weight.

Grain A particle of a mineral. Rocks can be described as fine grained or coarse grained depending on the size of the particle.

Greenhouse effect The process by which heat, radiated from the ground, is trapped by gases in the atmosphere, such as carbon dioxide, leading to global warming.

Groundmass see **matrix**

Hanging valley A tributary or small valley that enters a main valley on one of its sides and at a higher level. This occurs because the main valley has been eroded more deeply, usually by a glacier.

Horn A steep-sided mountain peak, formed by erosion by several glaciers.

Igneous rock A type of rock that forms as magma or lava cools and hardens. Intrusive igneous rock forms underground from magma; extrusive igneous rock forms on Earth's surface from lava.

Lava Molten rock that is forced out of a volcano during an eruption onto Earth's surface.

Luster The way a mineral shines. It is affected by light reflecting off the surface of the mineral.

Magma Molten rock that is deep underground, in Earth's mantle or crust.

Mantle The layer of Earth between the outer core and the crust. The mantle is made of solid rock that is very hot and slightly viscous, allowing it to flow and circulate over long periods of time.

Matrix The mass of rock in which larger crystals or fossils are embedded. Another word for matrix is groundmass.

Metamorphic rock A type of rock that has been changed by intense heat and/or pressure, causing physical and chemical changes as well as the partial melting and recrystallizing of its minerals.

Meteor A rock that burns up as it enters Earth's atmosphere, forming a shooting star.

Meteorite A rock from space that falls to Earth's surface without completely burning up.

Micrometeorite A microscopic meteorite.

Mineral A naturally occurring mixture of chemicals that has certain regular characteristics, such as atomic structure and chemical composition. Minerals are the building blocks of rocks.

Mohs scale A scale used to measure the relative hardness of minerals.

Ore A rock from which a metal is mined.

Period A division of geological time during.

Plate A large fragment of Earth's crust, also known as a tectonic plate.

Porous Solid matter containing a large number of tiny holes that let liquids or gases pass through.

Recrystallization The formation of new mineral grains in a rock while the rock is in a solid state.

Rock A solid mixture, or aggregate, of minerals. Rocks are divided into three main groups: igneous, sedimentary, and metamorphic.

Rock cycle The continuous cycle through which old rocks are transformed into new ones.

Scree A mass of loose rubble and gravel on a mountain slope, caused by weathering.

Sediment Mud, sand, or other particles that settle on the sea floor or other calm environment.

Sedimentary rock A type of rock that forms when sediment is compressed and cemented. The sediment may consist of eroded rock debris or of organic remains, such as the mineral shells of sea organisms.

Silica A hard mineral that is the main component of sand. It occurs naturally as quartz, and its chemical name is silicon dioxide.

Stalactite An icicle-shaped deposit of calcite hanging from the roof of a cave.

Stalagmite A deposit of calcite shaped like an upside-down icicle that rises from the floor of a cave.

Strata A sequence of rock formations that can tell a story of geological process over time.

Streak The color that a powdered mineral makes when rubbed across an unglazed tile.

Tectonic Of the landforms and rock masses created and affected by forces within the plates that make up Earth's crust.

Translucent Of a material that light is able to pass through, but that is not clear enough to look through.

Transparent Clear enough to look through.

Ultraviolet light An invisible form of radiation that has a shorter wavelength than visible light.

Viscous Of a thick and syrupy liquid—viscous liquids flow less quickly than runny liquids.

Volcano A vent or fissure in Earth's crust through which molten rock and hot gases escape. The molten rock typically piles up around the vent, forming a mountain.

Weathering The breaking down of rocks or minerals by way of dissolving or by crumbling into gradually smaller particles of force.

Index

The author would like to thank:
Richard Tayler for minerals and advice;
Susan Brown at Rockwatch
(www.rockwatch.org.uk) for ideas.

Model Jack Williams

Index Hilary Bird

**The publishers would like to thank the
following for their kind permission to
reproduce their photographs:**
a=above; b=below; c=center; l=left;
r=right; t=top
Alamy: /Jon Arnold Images/James
Montgomery: 31br; Ardea: /Bob Gibbons 45
(sea erosion), /Robyn Stewart 45br, /Francois
Gohier 49crb, /Kenneth W. Fink 52bl;
Collections: /Peter Wilson 10bl, /Paul Watts
44–45t, /Simon Warner 49tr, /David Bowie
65tr; Corbis: /Brenda Tharp 6bl, /Ron Watts
6bc, /Don Mason 7b, /Frank Lane Picture
Agency/Derek Hall 9–10t, /Roger Ressmeyer
12tr, /Eye Ubiquitous/Bennett Dean 12br, /

Lindsay Hebberd 13tc, /Patrik Giardino 13r,
/Sandro Vannini 13bc, /Tom Bean 13bl,
47tl, 48–49, /D.W. Peterson 18br, /Bettmann
33tr, /James Pomerantz 39tr, /Bob Krist
40bl, /ChromoSohm Inc, Joseph Sohm 55tl, /
James L. Amos 58–59t, /George H. H. Huey
62tr, /Annie Griffiths Belt 69br; Dorling
Kindersley: /courtesy Hunterian Museum
(University of Glasgow) 10c, /courtesy Natural
History Museum, London 10br, 20bl, 21l, 29br,
32b, 34 (bauxite, Illite, Corundum, Magnetite,
Fluorite), 55bl, 57tl, 59bra, 62br, 65bra, cr,
67br, /courtesy Royal Museum of Scotland
56–57c, /courtesy Naturmuseum
Senckenburg, Frankfurt 59bc; Moviestore
Collection: 67tr; NHPA:/Daniel Heuclin
44–45b, /James Warwick 45 (wind erosion),
/Otto Pfister 45bra; Science Photo Library:
/Dirk Wiersma 4c, 4–5t, /Bill Bachman 9br,
/Alan Sirulnikoff 11cr, /Lawrence Lawry
22br, /Andrew Lambert Photography
30bc, /Mike Agliolo 37tr, /Francoise Sauze
41tr. /Bernhard Edmaier 48bl, WG 65tc;
Still Pictures 17tr, 45tr, 49cra, 50bl,

61cra, /Josh Schachter 49br; University
of Southampton/Joe Kaplonek
(jtk@soton.ac.uk) 37bl;

**The publishers would also like to thank the
following photographers:**
Paul Bricknell, Jane Burton, Centaur Studios,
Andy Crawford, Mike Dunning, Andreas
Einsiedel, Lynton Gardiner, Steve Gorton,
Frank Greenaway, Graham High, Glenn L.
Huss, Colin Keates, Dinesh Khanna, Dave
King, Harry Taylor, Kim Taylor, Peter Wilson.

All other images © Dorling Kindersley.

For further information see:
www.dkimages.com